The Changing Seasons

Autumn

Paul Humphrey

FRANKLIN WATTS

LONDON•SYDNEY

First published in 2007
by Franklin Watts

© 2007 Franklin Watts

Franklin Watts
338 Euston Road
London NW1 3BH

Franklin Watts Australia
Level 17/207 Kent Street
Sydney, NSW 2000

A CIP catalogue record for this book is available from the British Library

Dewey classification number: 578.4'3

ISBN: 978 0 7496 7164 8

Planning and production by Discovery Books Limited
Editors: Paul Humphrey, Rebecca Hunter
Designer: Jemima Lumley

Photo credits: CFW Images/Chris Fairclough: back cover, 6, 8, 15, 18, 25; CFW
Images/EASI-Images/Ed Parker: 13; Corbis: 17 (Ashley Cooper/Pic Impact); Chris
Fairclough: front cover bottom, 9, 10, 11, 19, 22, 23, 24, 26; Getty Images: 7 (Benn
Mitchell), 21 (Altrendi Nature); 27 (Phillip Lee Harvey); Istockphoto.com: 12 (Nancy
Tripp), 14 (Pawel Kaminski), 16 (George Bailey), 20 (Andrey Grinyov), front cover
middle.

Printed in China

Franklin Watts is a division of Hachette Children's Books,
an Hachette Livre UK company.

Contents

Autumn starts 6

Falling leaves 8

Nuts and berries 10

Mist and dew 12

Ripe fruits 14

Autumn storms 16

Planting seeds 18

Birds and squirrels 20

Autumn games 22

Frosty weather 24

Winter is coming! 26

Autumn projects 28

Index 30

Autumn is the season that follows summer.

In autumn, the
weather changes
all the time.

7

The leaves turn red, yellow and brown.

They fall to the ground all around us.

There are chestnuts
on the trees ...

... and blackberries
in the hedgerows.

The mornings are colder. Dew forms on spiders' webs.

13

In the orchard,
the trees are
full of fruit.

Ripe apples are picked and sent to the shops.

There are often storms in autumn.

Trees can be blown down by strong winds.

17

Farmers plough their fields, ready for the new seeds.

19

Birds fly to warmer places.

Squirrels gather nuts and
acorns to eat in winter.

We start to play autumn games.

When it is wet outside, it is
fun to go swimming indoors.

At the end of autumn the weather turns colder.

The trees are bare and there can be frost on the ground.

It is time to dress up warmly ...

... for outdoor walks.
Winter is coming!

Autumn projects

A seed necklace

Many plants and fruits make seeds in the autumn.
You can make a lovely seed necklace from pumpkin seeds.

You will need:
Lots of pumpkin seeds 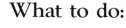 A thick needle
Some food dye in different colours 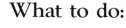 Jam jars full of water
Waxed dental floss 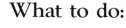 Scissors

What to do:
1. Add a teaspoon of food dye to the water in each jam jar.
2. Sprinkle a few pumpkin seeds into each jar and leave overnight.
3. Take out the seeds and leave them to dry.
4. Thread the large needle with dental floss.

5. Make a hole in the top of each seed and thread the dental floss through it.
6. Tie off the end of the dental floss to make your necklace.

A rain gauge

Autumn is often rainy. You can measure how much rain falls in autumn with this rain gauge.

You will need:
A large, clear plastic bottle ✿ Scissors or a sharp knife
A ruler ✿ Some bricks ✿ A notebook and pencil

What to do:

1. Ask an adult to cut the top off of the bottle and turn it upside down into the bottom half.

2. Stand the rain gauge outside where it will catch the rain. Support it with bricks to stop the wind blowing it over.

3. Measure how much rain falls in your rain gauge every day, or once a week, throughout the autumn. Don't forget to tip the water out once you have measured the rain.

4. Make a record of your results. When was it wettest?

Index

Apples   15

Birds   20
Blackberries   11

Chestnuts   10

Dew   12

Farming   18-19
Frost   25
Fruit   14-15

Games   22

Leaves   8-9

Nuts   21

Orchards   14-15

Ploughing   18-19

Rain gauge   29

Seeds   18-19, 28
Spiders' webs   12-13
Squirrels   21
Storms   16-17
Swimming   23

Trees   8, 14-15, 16-17, 24-25

Weather   7, 12, 16-17, 24-25